alone
together

Quarto is the authority on a wide range of topics.

Quarto educates, entertains and enriches the lives of our readers—enthusiasts and lovers of hands-on living.

www.quartoknows.com

First published in the United States in 2017 by
words & pictures, part of The Quarto Group
6 Orchard, Lake Forest, CA 92630

A CIP record for the book is available from the Library of Congress.

ISBN: 978-1-91027-728-7

1 3 5 7 9 8 6 4 2

Printed in China

alone together

clayton junior

words & pictures

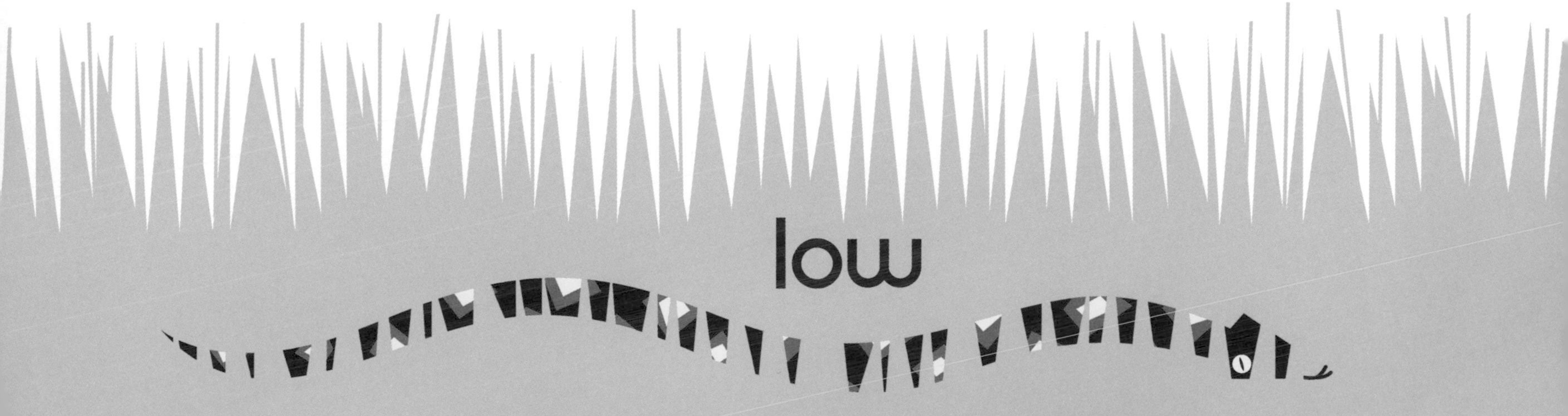
low

messy

tidy

LOUD

quiet

moving

still

far

close

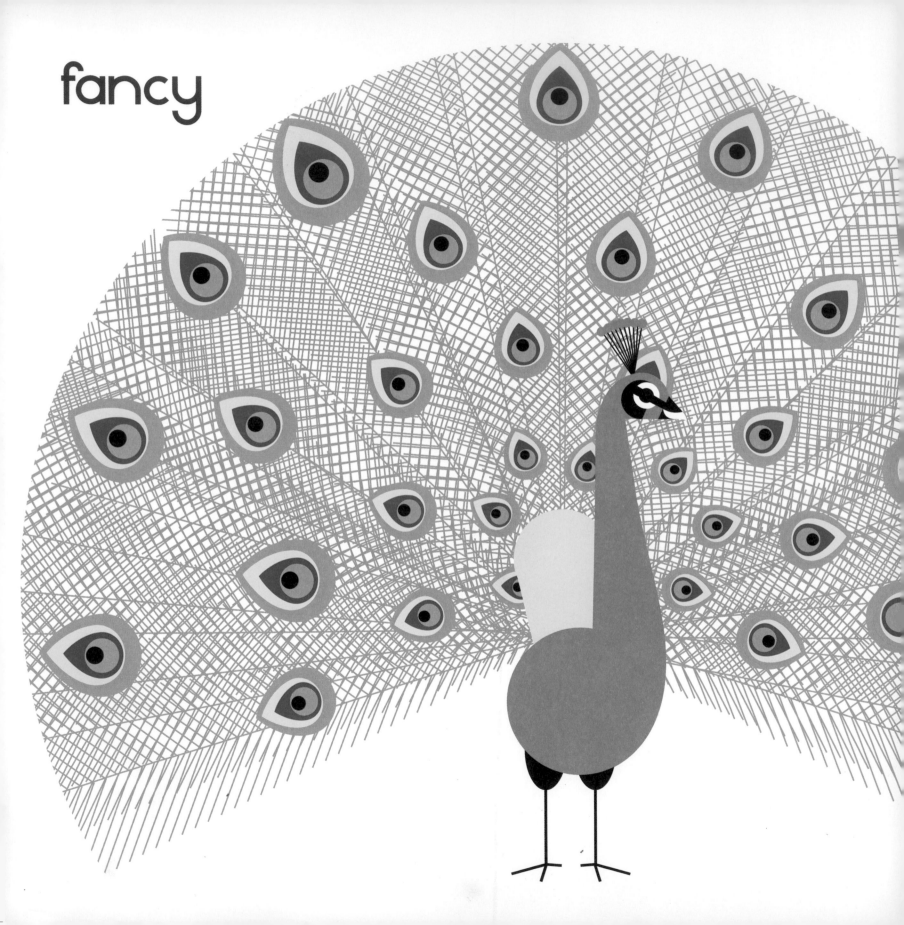

fancy

serious

slow

fast

alone

together

sturdy

fragile

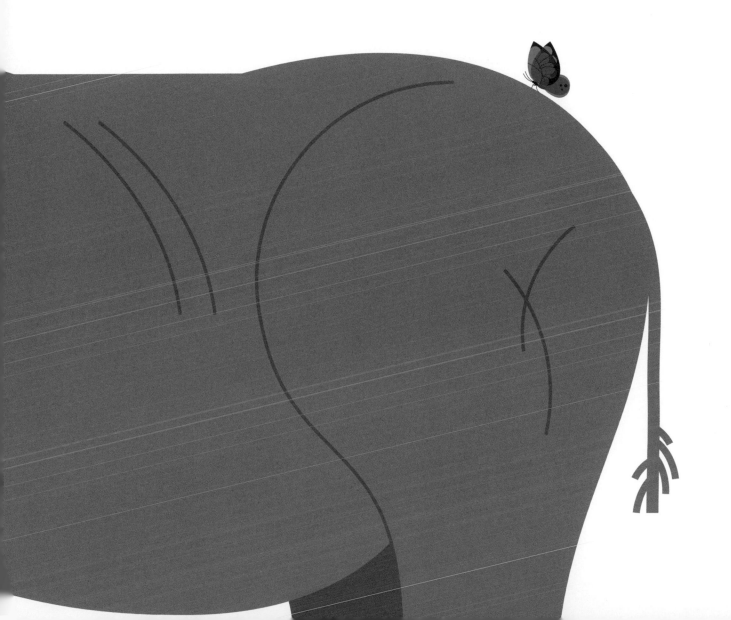

stripes

spots

spiky

soft

big

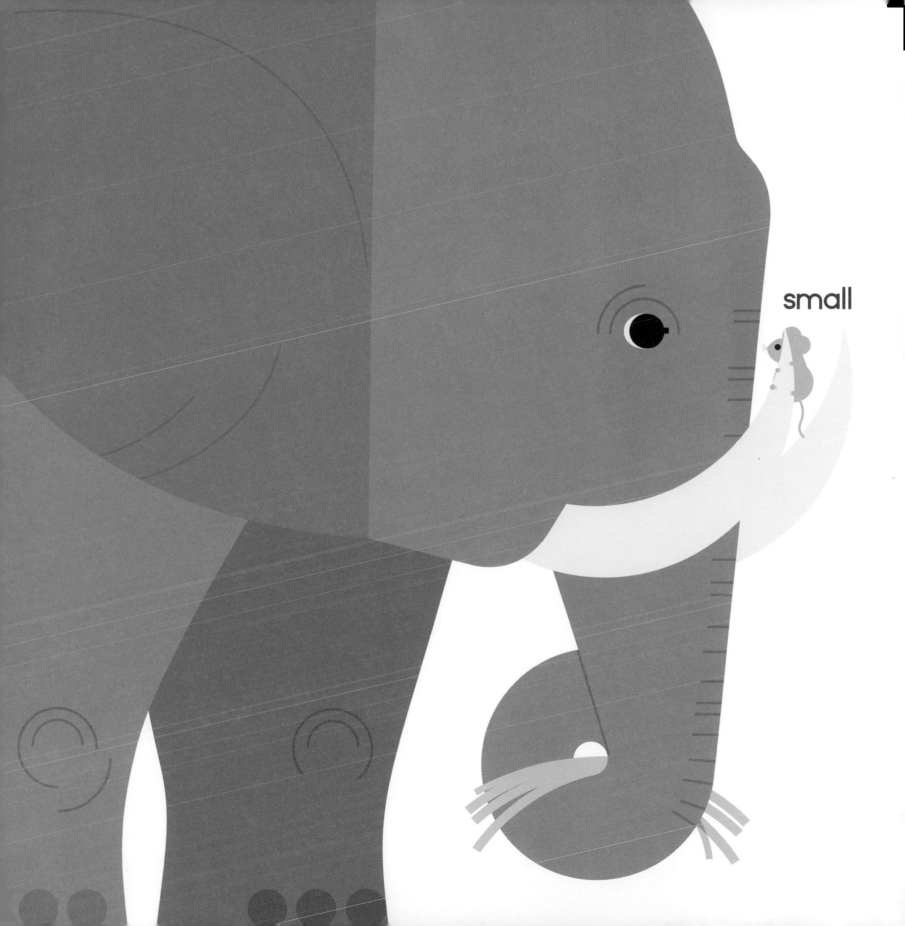

small

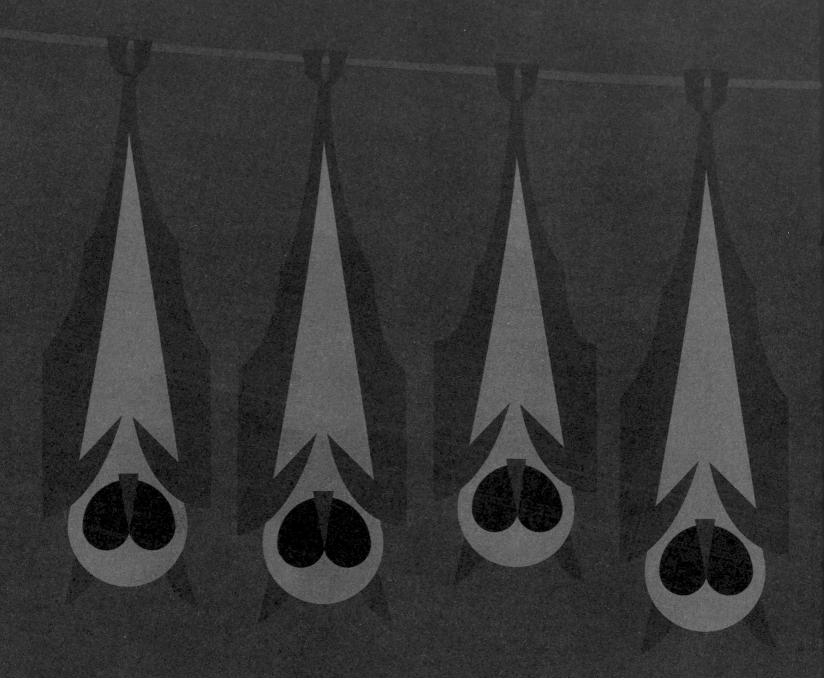

awake

captive

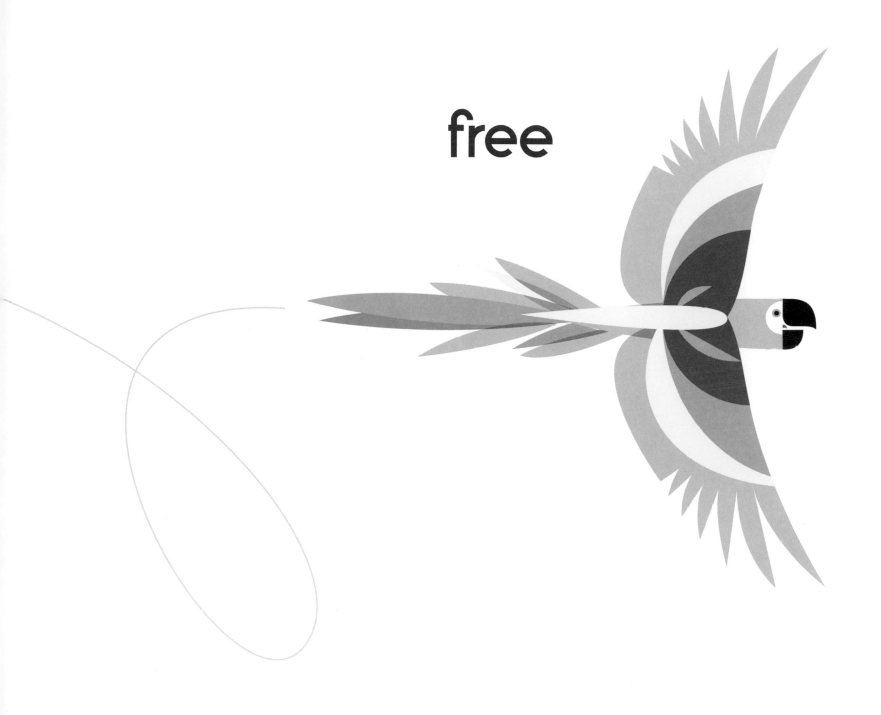